BASEBALL LEGENDS

Hank Aaron
Grover Cleveland Alexander
Ernie Banks
Albert Belle
Johnny Bench
Yogi Berra
Barry Bonds
Roy Campanella
Roberto Clemente
Ty Cobb
Dizzy Dean
Joe DiMaggio
Bob Feller
Jimmie Foxx
Lou Gehrig
Bob Gibson
Ken Griffey, Jr.
Rogers Hornsby
Walter Johnson
Sandy Koufax
Greg Maddux
Mickey Mantle
Christy Mathewson
Willie Mays
Stan Musial
Satchel Paige
Mike Piazza
Cal Ripken, Jr.
Brooks Robinson
Frank Robinson
Jackie Robinson
Babe Ruth
Tom Seaver
Duke Snider
Warren Spahn
Willie Stargell
Frank Thomas
Honus Wagner
Ted Williams
Carl Yastrzemski
Cy Young

CHELSEA HOUSE PUBLISHERS

BASEBALL LEGENDS

MIKE PIAZZA

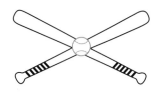

Brant James

Introduction by
Jim Murray

Senior Consultant
Earl Weaver

CHELSEA HOUSE PUBLISHERS
Philadelphia

Cover photo credit: AP/Wide World Photo

Produced by Choptank Syndicate, Inc.

Editor and Picture Researcher: Norman L. Macht
Production Coordinator and Editorial Assistant: Mary E. Hull
Designer: Lisa Hochstein
Cover Designer: Alison Burnside

1 3 5 7 9 8 6 4 2

Library of Congress Cataloging-in-Publication Data

James, Brant.
      Mike Piazza / Brant James; introduction by Jim Murray;
senior consultant, Earl Weaver.
        p. cm. — (Baseball legends)
      Includes bibliographical references and index.
      ISBN 0-7910-4379-7 (hc)
      1. Piazza, Mike, 1968- —Juvenile literature.
2. Baseball players—United States—Biography—Juvenile
literature. 3. Los Angeles Dodgers (Baseball team)—Juvenile
literature. I. Weaver, Earl, 1930- . II. Title.
III. Series.
GV865.P52J36 1997
796.357'092—dc21
  [B]   97-5504
                                                         CIP
                                                         AC

CONTENTS

WHAT MAKES A STAR

Jim Murray

No one has ever been able to explain to me the mysterious alchemy that makes one man a .350 hitter and another player, more or less identical in physical makeup, hard put to hit .200. You look at an A1 Kaline, who played with the Detroit Tigers from 1953 to 1974. He was pale, stringy, almost poetic-looking. He always seemed to be struggling against a bad case of mononucleosis. But with a bat in his hands, he was King Kong. During his career, he hit 399 home runs, rapped out 3,007 hits, and compiled a .297 batting average.

Form isn't the reason. The first time anybody saw Roberto Clemente step into the batter's box for the Pittsburgh Pirates, the best guess was that Clemente would be back in Double A ball in a week. He had one foot in the bucket and held his bat at an awkward angle—he looked as though he couldn't hit an outside pitch. A lot of other ballplayers may have had a better-looking stance. Yet they never led the National League in hitting in four different years, the way Clemente did.

Not every ballplayer is born with the ability to hit a curveball. Nor is exceptional hand-eye coordination the key to heavy hitting. Big league locker rooms are filled with players who have all the attributes, save one: discipline. Every baseball man can tell you a story about a pitcher who throws a ball faster than anyone has ever seen but who has no control on or *off* the field.

The Hall of Fame is full of people who transformed themselves into great ballplayers by working at the sport, by studying the game, and making sacrifices. They're overachievers—and winners. If you want to find them, just watch the World Series. Or simply read about New York Yankee great Lou Gehrig; Ted Williams, "the Splendid Splinter" of the Boston Red Sox; or the Dodgers' strikeout king Sandy Koufax.

A pitcher *should* be able to win a lot of ballgames with a 98-miles-per-hour fastball. But what about the pitcher who wins 20 games a year with a fastball so slow that you can catch it with your teeth? Bob Feller of the Cleveland Indians got into the Hall of Fame with a blazing fastball that glowed in the dark. National League star Grover Cleveland Alexander got there with a pitch that took considerably longer to reach the plate; but when it did arrive, the pitch was exactly where Alexander wanted it to be—and the last place the batter expected it to be.

There are probably more players with exceptional ability who didn't make it to the major leagues than there are who did. A number of great hitters, bored with fielding practice, had to be dropped from their team because their home-run production didn't make up for their lapses in the field. And then there are players like Brooks Robinson of the Baltimore Orioles, who made himself into a human vacuum cleaner at third base because he knew that working hard to become an expert fielder would win him a job in the big leagues.

A star is not something that flashes through the sky. That's a comet. Or a meteor. A star is something you can steer ships by. It stays in place and gives off a steady glow; it is fixed, permanent. A star works at being a star.

And that's how you tell a star in baseball. He shows up night after night and takes pride in how brightly he shines. He's Willie Mays running so hard his hat keeps falling off; Ty Cobb sliding to stretch a single into a double; Lou Gehrig, after being fooled in his first two at-bats, belting the next pitch off the light tower because he's taken the time to study the pitcher. Stars never take themselves for granted. That's why they're stars.

ONE OF THE BEST

"I'm really kind of choked up."
— Mike Piazza

Truth is sometimes more absurd than fiction, and Mike Piazza was about to craft a chapter not even the boldest of writers would dare to create.

The 27-year-old catcher stood at home plate in a white Los Angeles Dodgers home uniform, even though he was a continent away from Chavez Ravine and Dodger Stadium, leading off the second inning of the 1996 All-Star Game in Philadelphia. He had grown up in nearby Phoenixville, watching his Philadelphia Phillies heroes in this same Veterans Stadium. Twenty years ago he had seen his first big league game here, the 1976 All-Star Game. His hero, Phillies third baseman Mike Schmidt, had hit two home runs.

In pregame ceremonies Piazza was afforded a career highlight in a first-pitch ceremony involving Phillies Hall-of-Famers Schmidt, Steve Carlton, Jim Bunning, and Robin Roberts. Piazza was chosen to catch Schmidt's toss, and received an amazing gift as a result.

"It's hard to believe this," Piazza said in a television interview. "He wrote on the ball, 'Wishing you the best, I think you're the best.' Just to grow up and watch Mike Schmidt, a Hall of Fame third

Mike Piazza watches the flight of the ball he has just hit out of Philadelphia's Veterans Stadium to give the National league a 3-0 lead in the 1996 All-Star Game. Cleveland Indians pitcher Charles Nagy and Texas catcher Ivan Rodriguez also knew it was a home run as soon as it left the bat.

baseman, and try to emulate him and become a big league player . . . I'm really kind of choked up. I don't know what to say."

Piazza's world had seemingly come full circle. He had gone from a player-worshipping kid to a high school and junior college talent, to a player skipped over by every big league team, to National League Rookie of the Year, to the All-Star team. As he stood at home plate, a section full of Piazzas cheered wildly for him. Reporters packed into press boxes and photographers in camera wells all knew he was the perfect story: the hometown kid making good.

Piazza's All-Star selection was no fluke. He deserved this spot. His swing was not classic, but it produced results. His .356 batting average led the National League; he had belted out 22 homers and caught every day despite a knee injury suffered in June. He had gotten himself here through sheer will.

Piazza settled into the batter's box, gazing out at Cleveland Indians right-hander Charles Nagy on the mound. Nagy was the best the American League had to offer, boasting an 11–2 record.

Texas catcher Ivan Rodriguez signaled for a fast ball. Nagy tried to pump one past Piazza. He failed. The right-handed swinger thrust forward until his left leg planted in the soil like a javelin, his upper body twisting violently to bring his bat to bear on the pitch. The ball exploded off Piazza's bat as his uppercut hack finished above his head like an unorthodox golf swing.

Nagy knew it was gone. Piazza knew it was gone, and so did the 62,670 fans at "The Vet." Piazza's cannonade—his second consecutive All-Star homer dating back to his last at-bat in the

1995 midsummer classic—rose and rose through the damp Philadelphia air until it clanked off the concrete facade of the upper deck in left field 445 feet away.

The National League led, 3–0, and was on its way to its third straight All-Star win with a 6–0 triumph. In the third inning he sprayed a two-out double to right off California Angels' left-hander Chuck Finley that scored Cincinnati Reds shortstop Barry Larkin for a 4–0 lead and won for Piazza the All-Star Game Most Valuable Player Award.

After the game was over, as accolades were heaped upon him, he seemed stunned, humbled. When acting commissioner Bud Selig presented him with the MVP trophy, Piazza just smiled and said, "Thanks, Commish."

"Participating in this game is a tremendous honor," Piazza said. "To do pretty well is another thing. I'm choked up."

The MVP trophy looked good in Piazza's arms, but his prolonged poses for photographers looked strangely like a warm-up for a National League MVP ceremony as the All-Star evening quickly gave way to thoughts of the second half of the 1996 season. Many experts expected Piazza would earn the full-season honor as well.

All of these thoughts were like a waking dream in the silvery glow of the stadium lights, washed together from different periods of his life. Just a few miles from here his career had begun in a backyard batting cage. Hours of dedicated practice had made him a high school and American Legion standout.

That drive had made him a professional athlete despite all the doubts of scouts paid to discover players with talent and potential. He had begun the journey as a 62nd-round pick in 1988.

It had led him to the balmiest reaches of the Caribbean, a place that tested his will and hardened his intentions to succeed. He had seen the Northwest League, Florida State League, Mexican Winter League, California League, and Pacific Coast League. He had known hours and days and weeks of frustration and toil, learning to transform himself from a first baseman to a catcher. He had endured marathon bus rides with no showers, warm sodas, cold corn dogs, and constant nagging questions about why he was even in professional baseball.

Piazza's home run and double paced the NL to a 6–0 win and earned him the All-Star Most Valuable Player Award. "I'm choked up," he admitted when they handed him the trophy.

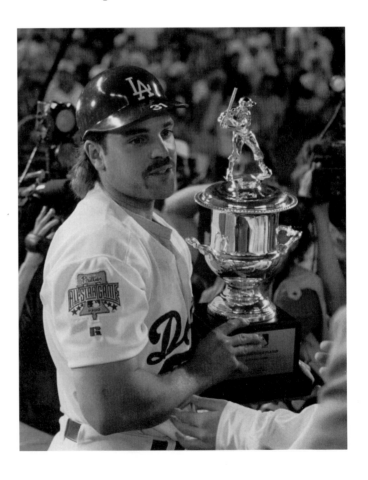

But this night was worth every ounce of energy he had exerted. Tonight of all nights, he knew he was a major leaguer. And that was all he had ever wanted to be.

2

UNWANTED HIGH SCHOOL STAR

"They didn't have anything positive to say."
— Mike Piazza

Y oung men and women are not necessarily destined for any particular path in life. The son of a welder can become a business tycoon and his son can become one of the greatest baseball players of his time. One thing makes it all possible: desire.

Michael Joseph Piazza was born September 4, 1968 in Norristown, Pennsylvania to Vince and Veronica Piazza. His father was a welder's son and high school dropout, who began in the used car business, invested successfully in real estate, and became a millionaire in a computer-service venture.

For as long as Mike could remember, he had one desire: to be a baseball player. He worked as hard to achieve that goal as his father had worked to succeed in life.

When Mike was 11, he and his father erected a ramshackle batting cage from various bits of wood in the backyard of their home on South Spring Lane in Phoenixville, a suburb of Philadelphia. That modest contraption soon became the center of young Mike's life. All year round, whatever the weather or time of day, Mike was in the batting cage, whacking pitches from his father

Ted Williams was one of baseball's greatest hitters. Tagged "The Splendid Splinter" when he was a tall lanky rookie in 1939, the Hall of Famer thumped a career .344 batting average with the Boston Red Sox between 1939 and 1960. When Mike Piazza was 16, his father arranged for Williams to visit the Piazza home and give Mike some batting tips.

or a pitching machine hour after hour. It was long, hard work, but a major league baseball player was under construction.

"I was out there every day," Piazza said. "I would come home from school, get a snack, watch cartoons, and then hit. Every spring I would see I was hitting the ball farther and farther."

Piazza made sure he was able to hit through the cold winter months of eastern Pennsylvania by shoveling snow out of the cage and heating the baseballs on a stove. A little pipe insulation around the handle of the bat buffered his hands from the brutal sting of a cold-weather knob-shot on aluminum.

His father eventually used some paneling to enclose the cage, and added the amenity of a heater. The cage became more functional, but it was even more of an eyesore.

"It was such an ugly thing," Vince Piazza said. "I can't believe the neighbors didn't complain. Actually, the zoning board came by once to investigate. When they asked what it was, I told them it was my son's ticket to the major leagues."

But it was Vince's connections that would eventually give Mike the chance to prove he belonged in the big leagues. Vince Piazza had a friend, Tommy Lasorda, the longtime manager of the Los Angeles Dodgers. They had grown up a few blocks apart in Norristown. Vince had idolized Tommy, the local baseball star, who was six years older. Wherever Tommy went, Vince was right behind him.

"I was his little buddy," Vince Piazza recalled. "We were inseparable, like family. Actually, my mother and his mother were fourth cousins."

Lasorda left Norristown to pursue a career in pro baseball. He became became one of the sport's most successful and revered managers, leading the Los Angeles Dodgers for 20 seasons before retiring July 28, 1996 because of heart problems. Vince Piazza and Lasorda remained close friends.

Mike worked as the visitors' batboy for the hometown Philadelphia Phillies during his summers, and was able to stroll through the Dodgers' clubhouse one year when they wrapped up the pennant at Veterans Stadium.

"That's what I want to do," Piazza said to himself, watching players cavort around the littered clubhouse. "I want to win a World Series. I want to be the champion."

His father's connections also helped Mike enjoy a personal visit with one of the greatest players in baseball history—Ted Williams. Vince Piazza and Williams had known each other for a couple of years, and the pair arranged to meet on a Saturday morning in 1984. Williams stopped by the Piazza home on his way to an appearance at a baseball card show in the Philadelphia area. Mike, then 16, wolfed down breakfast before getting some batting cage time and personal

Piazza chose third baseman Mike Schmidt as his boyhood hero. A three-time MVP and winner of 11 Gold Gloves, Schmidt slugged 543 home runs in 17 years with the Phillies. Here the future Hall of Famer is hoisted by his teammates after they won the 1980 World Series.

instruction from Williams. The thrilled family videotaped the session.

"I couldn't even talk because I was so nervous," Mike said.

Williams asked him, "Son, do you have my book on hitting?"

Mike smiled; he had memorized the book.

"Mike hits it harder than I did when I was 16," Williams told the family. "I guarantee you, this kid will hit the ball. I never saw anybody who looked better at his age."

Mike earned a spot as the first baseman on the Phoenixville High varsity baseball team in his junior year, and set the bi-county conference afire with his performance at the plate. He led the Phantoms to a 16–5 record with a .500 batting average, 28 runs scored, 38 RBI, and 12 homers. The next year he hit .442 with 11 home runs and 42 RBI, and was named the league's most valuable player.

"I remember the amount of time he dedicated to baseball," coach John "Doc" Kennedy recalled. "On the field he was always all business."

Piazza maintained contact with Kennedy and Phoenixville High throughout his early years in professional baseball, helping run a clinic one spring, and popping in for a team meeting.

"I was running the meeting and there was a knock at the door," Kennedy said. "I open the door and there's Mike. There were 38 to 40 kids in the room, and needless to say, he had a captive audience.

"It was really great. He talked to the kids for about 25 minutes about what it takes to make it in baseball, what they had to do. He sat around for the rest of the meeting while I ran it, and afterwards he signed anything anybody wanted in the school."

But in that summer of 1986, Piazza gener-
ated little interest from professional scouts. "Bird
dogs" look for certain tools when assessing raw
amateur talent: power, ability to hit for average,
speed, arm strength, and defense.

Mike's power was superb for high school, but
scouts did not project it well for the professional
ranks. His foot speed was woeful. His defense
was average; his batting average—good, but not
outstanding for preps—inspired no scouts.

"I have talked to a lot of scouts since then who
said they didn't like anything about me," Mike
said later. "They said that I couldn't run or hit."

Scouts looked for first basemen who were
either absolute mashers, or combined a .320-plus
batting average with outstanding defense. Mike
had a strong arm, but he seldom got to show it
at his position.

Coach Kennedy said, "I honestly can't say I
was surprised that the scouts overlooked him.
In high school he was a real skinny kid, not the
6-foot-3, 200-pounder he is now. I'd be surprised
if he was more than 165 then. Certainly scouts
look for foot speed, and Mike didn't demonstrate
that, so that was a negative factor. Scouts knew
he could hit, but they were wanting to know what
else he could do. In their minds a player had to
be able to do more than hit."

June came and went that summer without
any phone calls from major league teams. The
1986 amateur draft passed him by, so it was
now time to think of college. But college
recruiters had not been overwhelming him either.
No major baseball programs came calling for
his services.

Then Tommy Lasorda came to the rescue.

3

NEVER GIVE UP

"I asked the Dodgers to draft him as a favor."
— Tommy Lasorda

Despite his home run swing, baseball scouts ignored Piazza in high school. He was a slow runner and no glove man. So he went to Miami-Dade North Community College, where he played first base and showed flashes of power, but the scouts still passed him by.

The summer following Mike Piazza's graduation from high school was a critical time in the life of a would-be professional baseball player. He was 18, his stock, in the eyes of the scouting fraternity, was not good, and his shelf-life was expiring fast.

Tommy Lasorda called a friend of his, University of Miami head baseball coach Ron Fraser, and arranged for Piazza to land a spot on the Hurricane roster. Miami had one of the most successful and respected intercollegiate baseball programs in the country. The Hurricanes attracted the best high school talent; Piazza, despite all his hard work, was overmatched. In his freshman season he managed just one hit in nine at-bats as a back-up first baseman. Seeing his career languishing, he left the school and transferred to Miami-Dade North Community College to play for another close Lasorda friend, Demie Mainieri.

"Tommy sent him down to me after Miami," Mainieri, now retired, recalled. "I remember I was kind of annoyed he hadn't sent him to me initially."

Despite missing several weeks with a broken hand, Piazza hit a solid .364 that season, batting mostly fifth in the order, and helped the Falcons to a third-place finish in the Southern Conference. Some of Piazza's trademarks began to develop that year.

"He showed some flashes of power," Mainieri said. "And that was good considering our home park was 390 feet to the power alleys. I worked a lot with him trying to make him a very aggressive hitter, and he turned into an aggressive hitter. I think that's why he got so good at hitting in clutch situations."

Mainieri said he was shocked at how strong Piazza's throwing arm was, a bonus feature in a first baseman that eventually helped sell him as a catcher. But it was the intangibles, not simply the raw baseball abilities, Mainieri most remembered about his pupil.

"He was always a very positive, upbeat person," Mainieri said. "You can tell he really comes from a good family. They raised him right. He had incredible work habits; he was always the first one out there, and the last to leave.

"He was always a gentleman, an outstanding individual. He's somebody you like to see become a big success because he's just a super role model."

John Herrholz, a pitcher on that Falcons team with Piazza, and later Miami-Dade's pitching coach, said the slugger was most impressive in warmups.

"Everybody would stop and watch him in batting practice," he said. "More balls would end up on the other side of the fence than on his side. He didn't seem to hit them that far in games, though."

Herrholz added that Piazza's defense at first base was outstanding. "He was phenomenal," he said. "He was the first first baseman I ever played with that could do a complete split stretching for the ball."

Piazza's junior college career ended as a success, but he still failed to charm the scouts who had spurned him after high school.

"It's really a testament to Mike's determination that he kept going on," high school coach John Kennedy said. "No one seemed to want him, but he did not let that upset him. He continued with his determined attitude, and he was determined he was going to get his chance."

Thanks, again, to Lasorda, that chance came his way. Vince Piazza had often joked, maybe half-kiddingly, with Lasorda during those off-season chats about the Dodgers one day selecting his son in the draft. Now was the time. Lasorda arranged for the Dodgers to draft Mike as a favor to his friend, hopefully to help him gain offers from another four-year school.

The Dodgers did not want to waste a high selection on Piazza. They waited until the 62nd round, after 1,389 other young prospects had been chosen. Nobody in the media paid any attention to him. The Dodgers had done their manager a favor. Now they were in no hurry to follow up on it.

Mike did not hear from the Dodgers for two months, when he received a mailgram. Expecting to be assigned to a rookie league team, he was disappointed to learn that they wanted only to know where he would be attending school in the fall so they could keep track of his progress.

But Mike was not satisfied. He pleaded for a tryout.

Lasorda arranged for the workout at Dodger Stadium, with Ben Wade, then the club's scouting

Longtime Los Angeles Dodgers manager Tommy Lasorda and Mike Piazza's father were boyhood friends. As a favor, Lasorda arranged for the Dodgers to draft Mike. Here the effervescent Lasorda is losing an argument with umpires Jim Quick (center) and Bud Davidson.

director, and a batting practice pitcher on hand. Chavez Ravine echoed with the sound of wood mashing into leather.

"I just hammered balls into the blue seats," Piazza said.

Lasorda looked at Wade and asked, "If he was a shortstop who could hit balls into the seats like that, would you sign him?"

"Yes," Wade replied.

Lasorda probed again: "If he was a catcher who could hit balls into the seats like that, would you sign him?"

"Yes," Wade answered again.

"Then he's a catcher," Lasorda retorted.

Wade squirmed under Lasorda's arm-twisting manipulation, but finally agreed to watch Piazza make throws to second base.

"I threw as hard as I could," Piazza later recalled. "I think my arm is still hurting from that day."

Wade offered Piazza a $15,000 signing bonus.

"I said yes before he said thousand," Piazza said. "I would have done it for $15. I would have done it if he said I had to pay him $15,000."

Lasorda's eye for talent, and his absolute loyalty to a close friend, proved critical in the discovery of one of the greatest talents in modern baseball.

"I asked the Dodgers to draft him as a favor," Lasorda said. "And thank God they did."

4

MAKING IT

> "If I couldn't make it, I wanted it to be because I wasn't good enough, not because I didn't try hard enough."
> — Mike Piazza

Minor league baseball cruelly sorts out who will and who will not become major league ballplayers. Some players, upon making "The Show," look back upon the rigorous experience with a smile, as does a soldier who survived boot camp. Thousands of young men, gallantly chasing their dream, played hard, worked to improve, and hoped for a break. They played in small farming towns and mid-sized cities all across the land. Many grew homesick and dropped out. Few would make it to the big leagues.

Farm teams, especially those at the lower levels, run on threadbare budgets. Players often lived in tiny, dingy apartments. Dinner might be a cold corn dog and a cheeseburger on an all-night bus ride. Clubhouse showers sometimes spewed out cold water when they worked at all. Home was usually very far away, but loneliness was always close by.

Mike Piazza entered into this world as a willing participant. He knew it was up to him to make himself into a prospect. In the winter of 1988 he

When the Dodgers agreed to sign Piazza if he would be a catcher, Lasorda said to him, "You're a catcher." Piazza went down to the lowest minor leagues to learn the position.

Piazza plugged away in minor league ballparks resembling this rookie league field in Pikeville, Kentucky. He played in fall leagues and winter leagues, and in three years made it to the big leagues.

volunteered to go where no other American player had gone—to the Dodgers' camp for Latin players in Campo Las Palmas in the Dominican Republic.

Life in this remote corner of the Caribbean made the longest bus ride through the midwest seem like a luxury cruise. Piazza ate the same food every day for three months: two poached eggs, and something resembling ham for breakfast; chicken broth and two ham sandwiches for lunch; and beans and rice, with a little bit of bread, and sugar cane juice for dinner.

No one else spoke English, and his bunk was a regular gathering place for tarantulas. The experience hardened him, both physically and mentally.

"If I couldn't make it, I wanted it to be because I wasn't good enough, not because I didn't try hard enough," Piazza said. "I was going to give it everything I had, and if I wasn't good enough, so be it. But nobody really knows the bitterness, the adversity I went through."

He lost weight, but added muscle, and learned some Spanish, which would prove to be a major asset. He also became a skilled catcher.

In 1989 he began at the bottom of the Dodgers' farm system at Salem, Oregon in the rookie Northwest League. He batted .268 with 8 home runs in the short season, and made the All-Star team.

The next year he played his first "full" minor league season, and in the process played roughly 30 more games in a season than he ever had before. Still, he did not play every day. When a team spends a high draft pick on a prospect and then invests a million dollars or more in a bonus, they give that prospect the most playing time, and expect him to move up to the big leagues and start paying dividends in a hurry. Piazza had been drafted as an afterthought, a favor to somebody; nobody in the organization had a stake in his succeeding. If not for Lasorda's interest in him, he probably would have spent even more time collecting splinters on the bench.

His batting average slumped to .250, but he helped the Vero Beach Dodgers to the Florida State League championship, driving 20 doubles into the league's spacious outfields. He also struck out 68 times.

Piazza broke through as a slugger in his third year, leading all Dodger minor leaguers with 29 home runs at Bakersfield in the Class A California League. His swing became more refined and powerful. He batted .277 and drove in 80 runs. Attention was now being paid to him.

"You could just look at the guy and tell he could hit," said a rival manager in the league. "He could really hit the ball hard for that level."

Baseball America named him to their Class A All-Star team.

Piazza did not want to rest. He played at Mexicali in the Mexican Winter League, and hit .330 with 16 home runs. From there he reported to AA San Antonio, hit .377 in the first 31 games, and jumped to AAA Albuquerque of the Pacific Coast League. In the small ballparks and high-altitude cities of the circuit, he led the team with a .341 average, ran up a 25-game hitting streak, and bashed 16 home runs, and led all Dodger farmhands in total run production for the year.

The kid who had been drafted as a favor to their manager's friend had become the Dodgers' top minor league player. The long journey from the batting cage on South Spring Lane to Dodger Stadium was completed when Los Angeles called him up from Albuquerque on September 1, 1992. He caught a flight to Chicago for the last game of a three-game set with the Cubs at Wrigley Field. Arriving with the cobwebs of disbelief and weariness fuzzying his head, he discovered that he was in the starting lineup.

Determined to make the most of this day he had worked toward for so long, Piazza went 3-for-3, drew a walk, and made his first big league hit a fourth-inning double off right-hander Mike Harkey. He also threw out Dwight Smith trying to steal.

Piazza's first big league home run came 12 days later off Giants right-hander Steve Reed, a three-run blast into the right field pavilion at Dodger Stadium.

Piazza's wild ride wound down as the Dodgers failed to make the playoffs, and he finished his brief major league stint with a .232 batting average, 3 doubles, and 7 RBI in 21 games. Still disdaining rest, that fall he hit .291 with 3 homers and 23 RBI for the champion Sun Cities Solar Sox of the Arizona Fall League, a circuit created to showcase prized prospects.

He had gone from a kid nobody wanted to a "prized prospect" with a few years of hard work and dedication. Both Mike and Tommy were thankful for the small favor that Lasorda had once asked.

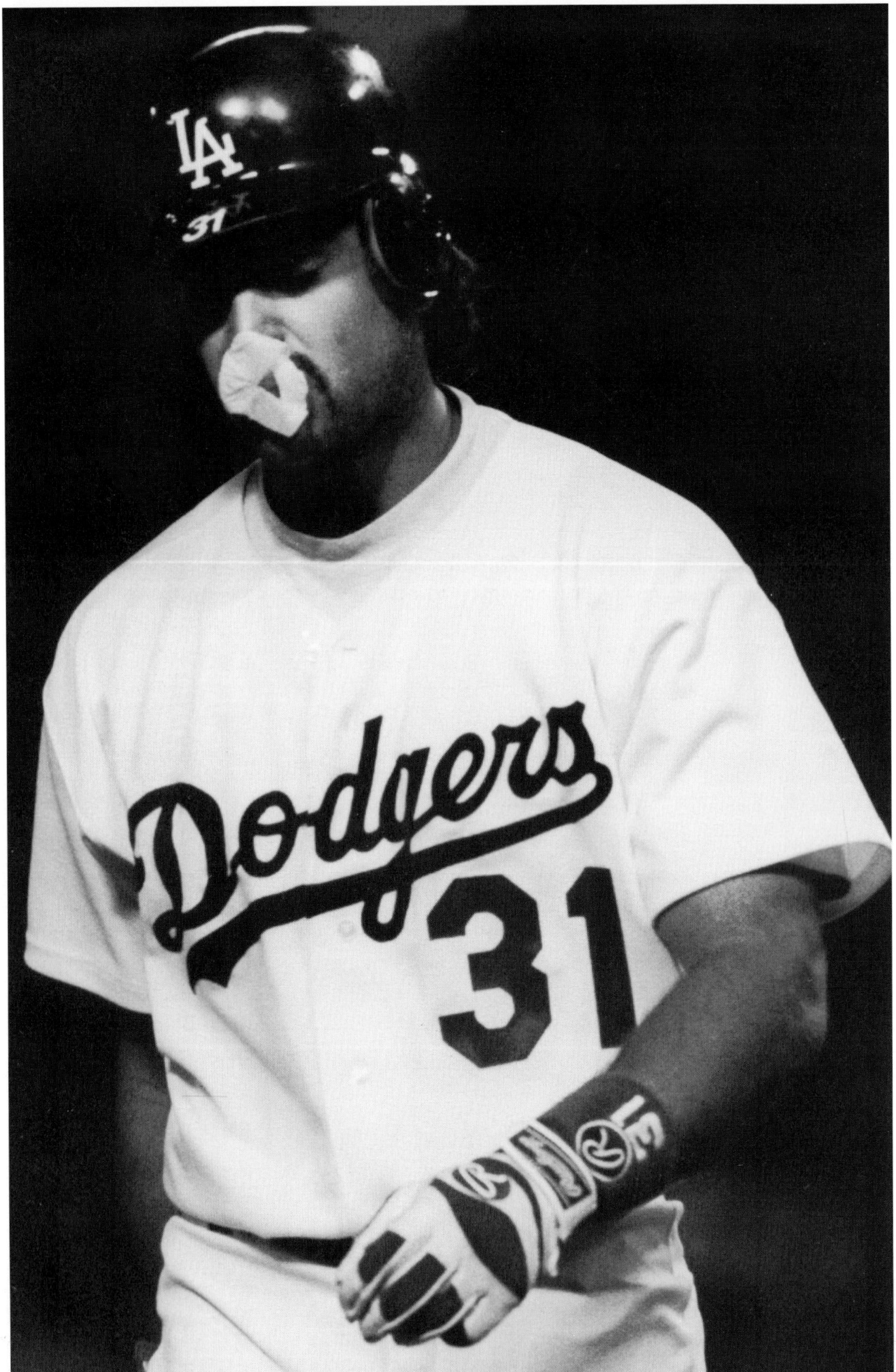
LA
31
Dodgers
31

5

ROOKIE OF THE YEAR

"I had to earn respect."

— Mike Piazza

The opportunity to prove himself came to Mike Piazza following the 1993 retirement of the Dodgers' popular and respected catcher Mike Scioscia. The 13-year veteran stepped down, clearing the path for Piazza to establish himself as an everyday big league catcher.

The job was Piazza's to win in spring training at Vero Beach, Florida. He outdueled Carlos Hernandez for the job with a hot hand. One day he was in the clubhouse after a "B" game in the Dodgers complex when the team needed a late-inning pinch hitter in the "A" game. He ran over to the field and blasted a monstrous home run. In another game he dove across the plate to poke at an Orel Hershiser slider, and was promptly knocked down by the next pitch.

You can't be a hero every time at bat. Piazza bursts his bubble gum as he walks back to the dugout after striking out with the bases loaded.

A pitcher would not have sent such an eye-opening message had he not deemed the batter a real threat at the plate. "I ended up getting a hit off him, and he says, 'Save something for the season,'" Piazza said.

Piazza became the first rookie to start in the Dodgers' opening day lineup since the team had moved from Brooklyn to Los Angeles in 1958. Winning the starting job involved not only performing on the field, but being able to maintain sanity against a constant barrage of personal questions from reporters. He was especially irked by questions about his father. Mike's father attracted publicity, and Mike could not escape the fallout, although he preferred to let his bat do the talking for him.

Vince Piazza had led a group of investors who submitted a bid of $115 million to purchase the San Francisco Giants and move the team to St. Petersburg, Florida. The bid was rejected by Major League Baseball because two members of the group reportedly failed a background security check. The elder Piazza, enraged by Major League Baseball's refusal to allow the purchase—and the later approval of a $100 million sale to another group—filed a discrimination suit.

Then there were the stories that Mike was really Tommy Lasorda's godson, and favoritism, not performance, had won him a place on the team. In fact, it was Mike's 11-year-old brother, Tommy, who was Lasorda's godson, not Mike.

All the gossip and speculation and the never-ending questions angered the young catcher. "Like I don't deserve to be here?" he asked. "Like Tommy's doing me a favor by letting me be on the team? Like all of this was done with mirrors?"

Just as pitchers like Hershiser were quick to test Piazza, so too were they quick to work with him, because his efforts behind the plate directly affected their success. A good catcher must be able to frame pitches effectively, pulling balls into the strike zone to fool umpires into thinking they were strikes. Catchers need to call the right pitches in certain situations, and earn the confidence and respect of their pitchers.

"I had to earn respect, no doubt about it," Piazza said. "The pitchers kind of took me under their wing. I would always talk to them when I wasn't playing. I learned their personalities and the way they think on the mound."

Piazza helped himself earn the respect of his pitching staff by throwing out 11 of the first 15 runners who attempted to steal against him in 1993. At one point in April Piazza caught seven consecutive runners—six of them St. Louis Cardinals. Piazza finished the season with a 35 percent throw-out ratio, third best in the National League. Opposing base stealers and managers wanted to see for themselves what Piazza could do; he was tested 166 times that year, most in the majors. His 58 runners caught set a Dodgers record.

As much as he was learning, he did have some tough moments, especially since the pitching staff included a knuckleballer, Tom Candiotti. The knuckleball, when thrown properly, flutters, dances, and tumbles toward the plate like a Wiffleball in a backyard game. Gripped with the fingernails, the pitch can change directions at any moment, dipping left or right, or both. Even experienced, agile catchers disdain catching it, and for the inexperienced Piazza, the task was arduous.

Piazza committed 14 passed balls in his rookie year, four in one game on June 12 at San Diego. Three of them happened with Candiotti on the mound.

"He put a lot of pressure on himself early because he really wanted to do well," Candiotti said.

An episode earlier in the season had helped to demonstrate both Piazza's intensity and his frustration with the knuckler. In a May 31 game against the Cards, Piazza lunged for a low Candiotti knuckler as Ozzie Smith attempted to steal second base. Piazza smothered the ball and fired an off-balance throw toward second, but his throw missed, instead plunking Candiotti on the butt. Players from both teams broke into laughter, but not Piazza, who began cursing.

"He takes everything so seriously," his roommate Eric Karros said. "We were winning 5-0, so who cares? Jeez! It was funny."

The next afternoon the entire Dodgers pitching staff arrived in the dugout with targets stuck to the seats of their pants.

"He still felt pretty bad about it," Candiotti said. "He said to me, 'What if I had hit you in

Hall of Fame catcher Roy Campanella, paralyzed by an automobile accident, worked with young catchers at the Dodgers' spring training camp in Vero Beach, Florida. "Campy told me to ignore other people's expectations and have fun playing the game," Piazza recalled.

the arm?' Catching is not a casual thing to him. If I lose a game, he feels like he let me down."

Piazza didn't let the Dodgers down often in 1993, earning N.L. Player of the Week accolades a season-record three times. His first honor came the last week of April. He embarked on a 10-for-23 (.435) binge with a double, 4 homers, and 8 RBI to earn the honor again June 14–20, and hit .458 with 4 doubles, 3 homers, and 10 RBI to secure the Sept. 27–Oct. 3 plaque.

Piazza was becoming a household name by mid-summer 1993, and he became the fourth senior circuit rookie catcher ever named to the All-Star team. He had hit 18 home runs at the break, and was invited to participate in the annual home run derby. Seattle's Ken Griffey, Jr., and Texas' Juan Gonzalez dominated that slugfest at Baltimore's Oriole Park at Camden Yards, which helped mask the embarrassing fact that Piazza was the lone participant not to whack a ball over the fence. Piazza went 0-for-1 and struck out in the All-Star game the next night.

That brief injection of humility did not temper his fantastic season, however, and he blistered the National League at a .320 batting clip the rest of the season to finish at .318. He drove in 112 runs and hit 35 home runs, the most ever by a rookie catcher. The two most memorable round-trippers of the year came in a year-end 12-1 win over arch-rival San Francisco that knocked the Giants out of the playoffs.

Piazza was also gaining a reputation for clouting majestic blasts; 17 of his drives traveled at least 400 feet, with the longest sailing 466 feet. Atlanta manager Bobby Cox said, "I have never seen anybody like him for hitting home runs to the opposite field. I'd say he does it 90 percent of the time. He has phenomenal strength."

But Piazza really went big-time, and became a cult hero to the slow-footed but big-hearted everywhere when he starred in a humorous commercial for ESPN's Sportscenter. In his personal "Sportscenter highlight" Piazza stole home to win the game for the Dodgers as the crowd, and his grandmother watching on television, cheered him on.

All the numbers and newfound commercial fame added up to one irrefutable conclusion: on October 27 Piazza became the 1993 National League "Jackie Robinson Rookie of the Year" winner as named by the Baseball Writer's Association of America. The Silver Slugger Award,

The catcher's position requires someone who can be part field general, game caller, pitcher calmer, plate blocker, and acrobat. Here Piazza lunges but misses the tag on Barry Bonds.

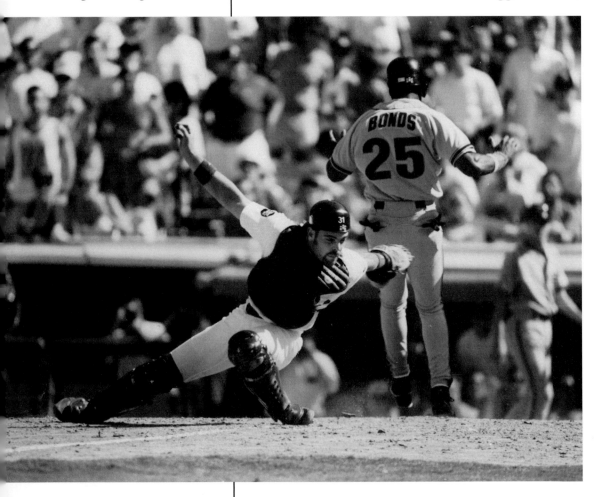

given to the best-hitting player at each position, followed, and he spent the winter collecting trophies. But he knew it would take still more hard work to make the next leap to becoming a genuine star. Many outstanding rookies never equaled their early success; Piazza did not intend to be one of them.

6

STARDOM

"He's the best hitter I ever played with."
— Brett Butler

Mike Piazza became a rookie of the year in 1993, but he became a star in 1994. Exhilarated by the abilities this most unusual of all beings— a hard-hitting catcher—possessed, and excited by the charisma and genuine warmth that he exuded, baseball fans, especially young ones, began clamoring for more and more of the second-year player.

It became ironic and sad later in that 1994 season that much of Piazza's charm had to be expressed away from the baseball field, helping Major League Baseball repair the inexorable marks left from a players' strike that wiped out the World Series for the first time in 90 years.

Piazza refused to be harmed by the dreaded, sometimes self-fulfilling "sophomore slump." He put to rest any thoughts of that nonsense when he started spring training with a pronounced bang. In his first at-bat of the Dodgers' third exhibition game he stroked a 450-foot homer. In his next time up he one-handed another home run over the left field fence.

He continued to mash balls into the horizon thereafter with 24 in just 107 regular-season

In 1996 Piazza caught the most international pitching staff in baseball: Japanese, Korean, Dominican and Mexican as well as American. Here, Hideo Nomo, the first Japanese player to star in the U.S., reaches toward the sky in his unique windup. Nomo won 16 games in 1996.

Piazza breaks his bat but still muscles a hit to drive in a run against the Mets in a late-season game in 1995.

games before play was halted on August 12 because the players and club owners could not work out their differences in the terms of their working agreement. Piazza batted .319, scored 64 runs, drove in 92, and was one of several players having marvelous offensive seasons, including Cleveland's Albert Belle and Seattle's Ken Griffey, Jr., who were on record-setting paces. Piazza established himself as the Dodgers' number one slugger and run producer, and began to close in on the team's all-time leaders.

Piazza's numbers put him in the All-Star Game, where he went 1-for-4 in a game that was much more subdued than midsummer classics past. Played in dreary Three Rivers Stadium in Pittsburgh, the game was perceptibly affected by the ever-looming reality of the coming strike.

The protracted stoppage was just a month away, and players and managers alike were now being inundated every day with more questions about impasses and strikes than balls and strikes. Baseball shut down on August 12 until May of the following season when a federal judge's order unwound the gnarled, bitter mess the negotiations had become.

Baseball, and players like Mike Piazza, were sunk into a morass of helplessness and bitter public opinion. Piazza kept himself busy, sane, and in shape as if the strike were an extended off-season. He lifted weights, worked out, and kept hitting, hitting, hitting. An avid fan of heavy metal music and guitar-playing, he used some of his free time to pursue another curiosity—acting.

He appeared on "Baywatch," "Married...With Children," and the soap opera "The Bold and the Beautiful" in 1994. He also became a fixture in the annual Homeboys vs. Awayboys tilt, the MTV "Rock & Jock" softball game.

Piazza began acting more and more during off-seasons his next two seasons in the next two years. He read for a part in the RobertDeNiro/ Wesley Snipes motion picture *The Fan*. The role he sought was that of a major league catcher. But somebody decided that he wasn't quite right for the part.

It seemed to him he had heard that before, from some baseball scouts. "I mean, I'm not Master Thespian even if I have done a Baywatch," he said. "But I'm not convincing enough to play a catcher? Come on."

Baseball's bleak winter ended with the stroke of a judge's pen in April 1995, and Mike Piazza greeted it with a stroke of his bat. The man who still spent holidays at his parents' home crushing baseballs in a batting cage, who vacationed near gyms to stay in shape, was ready when play began.

Piazza had often said his mind would not let him rest until he reached a higher level, and in 1995 the mind and body were both churning full force, although the body had a tough time staying healthy. He emerged as the Dodgers' all-time top slugger, batting .346, second only to perennial batting champion Tony Gwynn. He hit 32 home runs and drove in 92 runs. He also produced a .400 on-base percentage, giving him an uncommon mix of power, base-reaching and run-producing abilities.

"He's the best hitter I ever played with," Dodgers center fielder Brett Butler said. "Forget his power. Here's a guy who can't run a lick, and he's chasing Tony Gwynn for the batting title. I played with Dale Murphy, whom I consider a great hitter, and he hit for power and average on occasion. But not always. Piazza is ridiculous."

These feats were accomplished despite various injuries, including a strained hamstring, a severe contusion on his left wrist, and a torn ligament in his thumb that cost him 35 games. The Dodgers won 14 and lost 20 in his absences.

Piazza made his annual trip to the All-Star Game, combining with teammate Hideo Nomo as the starting battery. His lone hit was a game-tying home run.

Nomo, the so-called "Tornado" because of his tight, twisting windup, was a key part of a talented pitching staff that made Piazza's job difficult. He had to be as much a United Nations interpreter as a big league catcher. On any given day, on any given trip to the mound, he might have to deal with and communicate with Nomo, the Japanese Rookie of the Year; Ismael Valdes of Mexico; the Dominicans Pedro and Ramon Martinez; or, later, Chan Ho Park from Korea.

During one game Piazza walked to the mound and began speaking Spanish to the Japanese hurler. Nomo stared at him, puzzled.

"Brain cramp," Piazza later admitted.

Sometimes, the mix of players from different backgrounds became volatile. One of the game's traditional ways of hazing a rookie was to go into his locker during a road game, tear up or hide his clothes, and replace them with some outlandish get-up that he had to wear going home. Once, when they did it to Chan Ho Park, he went into a tantrum, threw a plate of food and a chair, yelled and cursed and demanded to know who was responsible for destroying his suit. His teammates tried without success to explain that it was all a joke. Park went to the airport wearing his uniform pants and a warmup jacket, still seething. When the prank was explained to him the next day, he calmed down and apologized.

"It's sad," Piazza commented. "It's like tradition is gone. I don't care if you understand or don't understand, you got to do it."

Catchers are urged to concentrate on their defensive duties first, but Piazza's work behind the plate did not detract from his hitting. He logged a career-high 49 multi-hit games and twice homered in three consecutive games. His biggest home run was a two-run shot on September 30 that helped clinch the National League West championship for the Dodgers and put them in the playoffs. But the Cincinnati Reds swept them and sent them home.

The joy of reaching the playoffs was quickly overcome by the disappointment of their quick exit. But Tommy Lasorda's enthusiasm for Piazza could not be dimmed.

"This guy's awesome," he said. "No catcher in the history of major league baseball has ever hit 91 home runs in his first three seasons.

Sometimes cultures clash. When some Dodgers played a traditional prank on Korean rookie pitcher Chan Ho Park, Park became upset and threw a tantrum.

Nobody has ever done it, and he's done it in two abbreviated seasons. He lost 21 games to injury [in 1995], and 18 because of the strike, In '94 he lost another 42 games because of the strike. So he's missed 80-some games in two years and this guy has more home runs in his first three years than any other catcher in the game."

7

THREE AND OUT AGAIN

"It's painfully obvious this team has some shortcomings."

— Mike Piazza

Stung by their rapid ouster from the 1995 playoffs, the Dodgers went into spring training in 1996 declaring that nothing short of a World Series appearance would satisfy them. Individual records and awards were fine, but they were not the ultimate goal for the young team. They assured their fans that they would do their best to go all the way this time.

Then things happened. In April Piazza suffered a slight tear in a knee ligament in a game in Philadelphia. Catching is a punishing position; squatting for hours, popping up quickly to make throws, and bracing for collisions at home plate are all part of the day's work. The legs and knees take a beating, and playing with injuries affecting them is bound to hamper a catcher. Piazza's painful knee forced him to the sidelines from time to time; he missed 12 games altogether.

In May Brett Butler, their leadoff batter skilled in bunting and getting on base, was diagnosed with tonsil cancer. He missed most of the season, but miraculously recovered enough to get back into the lineup in September.

Piazza grimaces as he tries to tag the Mets' Joe Orsulak who scored on a grounder. The punishment inflicted on a catcher's knees, hands and shoulders prompted the Dodgers to consider moving Piazza to first base.

They played for five weeks without shortstop Greg Gagne and opening day pitcher Ramon Martinez.

In June Tommy Lasorda, the 68-year-old manager who had led the Dodgers for 20 years, was felled by a heart attack. The ebullient, demonstrative Lasorda, whose blood was said to run Dodger blue, recovered and tried to return to the dugout, but a month later he resigned.

"For me to get into a uniform again—as excitable as I am—I could not continue," he said, fighting back tears. "I decided it's best for me and the organization to step down."

For the Dodgers, noted for the stability of their organization, former shortstop Bill Russell, who had been with them for 30 years, became only their third manager in more than 40 years. For Mike Piazza, the departure of the man who had coaxed the Dodgers into giving him a chance was an emotional jolt.

Amazingly, the physical and emotional traumas did not slow down Piazza's bat. He had long since dismissed the notion that his spectacular early years were a fluke. The question now was how high he could take his game. Swinging away with confidence almost as if he knew what was coming on every pitch, he powered 36 home runs and batted .336, third in the league. His home run in the All-Star Game in Philadelphia and his selection as the game's Most Valuable Player fulfilled a fantasy for him in the ballpark where he had worshiped the Phillies as a youngster.

The Dodgers were locked in a three-way fight for the NL West title with San Diego and the Colorado Rockies. They caught fire in late August

Piazza hugs his benefactor, Tommy Lasorda, after the manager gave a farewell speech to the fans at Dodger Stadium on July 30, 1996. Heart problems forced Lasorda to retire from managing after 20 years at the helm of the Dodgers, who had only two managers in the 38 years since the team moved from Brooklyn to Los Angeles in 1958.

and won 19 of 24, aided by Piazza's 19-game hitting streak. He jumped ahead of Tony Gwynn in the batting race, aiming to become the first NL catcher to win a batting title in more than 50 years.

Although he made only nine errors behind the plate, baserunners ran on him and his pitchers. They allowed 155 stolen bases, the most in either league.

Then, as September wore on, he wore down, and the Dodgers sank with him. His gimpy knee had never had a chance to rest and heal properly. There was nobody else in the lineup to pick him up; the Dodgers had the lowest slugging percentage in either league. They took a two-game lead into the final three-game series at home against the Padres that would decide the finish; the winner would face the Central champion St. Louis Cardinals, the loser would get the wild card spot and have to play the world champion Atlanta Braves in the first round. A victory for the Dodgers would probably also make Piazza the favorite to win the league's Most Valuable Player award. Those who vote on the award tend to choose players from winning teams.

All they had to do was win one of the three games. But they lost them all. "It's painfully obvious this team has some shortcomings," Piazza said, "and it was exploited in these last three games."

As an individual season, it was in some ways the best of his career. But it was one he might have trouble recalling fondly. A Los Angeles Times columnist, Mike Downey, summed it up: "From a high of being the All-Star Game's most valuable player, he finds himself, in virtually a week's time, seeing the National League's MVP award, batting title, and pennant slipping through his gnarled fingers."

(San Diego third baseman Ken Caminiti was the unanimous MVP choice; Piazza was second.)

The Braves brought their vaunted pitching staff—the best in baseball—to Los Angeles for the first two games of the division series. Both games were pitchers' duels, and both went to the visitors. Atlanta catcher Javy Lopez hit a 10th-inning home run to win Game 1, 2–1. A long fly ball by Piazza just failed to go out.

"He seemed to have crushed his," Piazza commented. "I seemed to have missed mine."

The Braves hit three solo home runs in Game 2 to edge the Dodgers, 3–2.

In Game 3 in Atlanta, Los Angeles ace Hideo Nomo gave up five runs early and the Dodgers could not come back. Early in the game Piazza had desperately tried to spark the team. After Todd Hollandsworth doubled off Tommy Glavine, Piazza flared a single to right field. Expecting Hollandsworth to score, he made a wide turn at first base. But Hollandsworth stopped at third. Piazza got caught in a rundown between first and second. When Hollandsworth broke for home, the Braves' Mark Lemke fired home and got him.

"I was trying to make something happen," Piazza said. "If there was a play at the plate, I didn't want to be standing at first base. That's bad baserunning, too. It was a gamble, and it didn't work out."

Piazza had a shot at redemption in the eighth inning with the Dodgers trailing, 5–1. With two men on base, he lined a pitch toward the right field foul pole, but Jermaine Dye made an outstanding running catch at the wall in foul territory. The Braves won, 5–2, and for the second year in a row the Dodgers bowed out of the playoffs without a win.

"Unfortunately, we kind of fizzled out," Piazza said. "It's embarrassing when you don't go out there and give them a little more fight."

In November Piazza joined an All-Star team that traveled to Japan for an eight-game series against Japanese stars. Despite the presence of legends like Cal Ripken, Jr., Barry Bonds and Brady Anderson, Piazza drew the most enthusiastic crowds and was in the greatest demand for interviews and promotions because he was the catcher for Japan's baseball hero, Hideo Nomo. When Piazza and Nomo held baseball clinics with other local players, he was surprised by the reception the youngsters gave him.

"I went up to talk and they all stood up straight, took their hats off and bowed their heads. I'm like, 'Who's here?'"

After signing a contract to endorse a Japanese bulldozer and other heavy machinery, Piazza visited the company's headquarters in Tokyo, where more than 500 employees cheered him.

"It was insane," he said. "I kind of felt like Elvis and Michael Jackson rolled up into one."

But he was still the plain, unchanged Mike Piazza from Phoenixville: he hit a home run in the Tokyo Dome, and he donated the cash award he received as "man of the game" to a Japanese children's charity.

THE STUFF OF LEGENDS

"The key to this game is consistency."
— Mike Piazza

Four years does not make a career, nor a case for the Hall of Fame. But in his first four years in the major leagues Mike Piazza put up offensive numbers that led observers to compare him with the catching legends of baseball: Johnny Bench, Mickey Cochrane, Roy Campanella, Yogi Berra, Bill Dickey—Hall of Famers all.

Only Campanella, who had starred for the Dodgers in the 1940s and 1950s back in Brooklyn, and Bench, the leader of Cincinnati's Big Red Machine of the 1970s, had hit as many as 30 home runs three times in their lengthy careers. Piazza did it three times in his first four years, and was stopped at 24 in the strike-shortened 1994 season.

Mickey Cochrane, the star catcher for the Philadelphia Athletics and Detroit Tigers in the 1920s and 1930s, held the record career batting average for catchers at .320. Through 1996 Piazza had a .326 average.

But the legendary catchers of the past had made it to Cooperstown with their mitts as well as their bats, and Piazza knew he had to work on that part of his game.

Roy Campanella set the standard for all Dodger catchers to come. Built like a fireplug, he was quick on his feet and swung a powerful bat. Campy was the NL MVP three times in five years in the 1950s. Always genial, a favorite of fans and players alike, he remained a coach with the Dodgers until he died in 1993.

"I believe I need to improve in every area of my game," he said. "The key to this game is to be consistent. All I can do is come out every day and work hard.

"It's nice to be mentioned among some of the best catchers. But I'm only in my fourth year and I have a long way to go before I can be compared to guys like Bench."

When a magazine asked him to pose with pictures of Campanella and Bench, he turned them down. Whatever others might say about him, he knew it was premature for him to consider standing alongside those Hall of Famers.

At 28, Piazza could look forward to many more productive years. But there was another reason he might never join the ranks of the top catchers. Catchers take a beating like no other position. Stubbed fingers, cuts and bruises from blocking pitches in the dirt and onrushing baserunners at the plate, worn out knees, dirt in the eyes, and the ever-dangerous foul tips

Hall of Fame catcher Mickey Cochrane, shown here leaping through the air to tag a sliding runner, has the highest career batting average for catchers: .320. Cochrane starred for the Philadelphia Athletics and Detroit Tigers in the 1920s and 1930s. Through 1996 Piazza was batting .326.

caroming off their heads and arms and legs are all part of the daily wear and tear on a catcher.

To preserve the health of their top slugger, the Dodgers considered moving Piazza to the relative safety of first base as the 1997 season got under way. The irony of such a switch was not lost on Piazza; he had started out as a first baseman, where he had drawn no interest from scouts who thought he wouldn't hit enough, and had been forced into catching to get a contract from the Dodgers, who might now convert him back to his original position to protect his offensive abilities.

With all his success, Piazza remained virtually unchanged as a person. While the spotlight and headlines often went to athletes who got into trouble, the good guys seldom made news. Piazza's squeaky-clean image was backed up by his charitable activities and clean living. It was appropriate that one of his endorsements was a shampoo for squeaky-clean hair.

Those who knew him before he became a star or even a professional ballplayer recognized how little he had changed. Jay Rokeach, the public address announcer for the Florida Marlins and sports information director at Miami-Dade North, remembered the young student whom nobody thought had a chance.

"We were all shocked when he signed, and then was in the big leagues. You never would have seen that coming. But the thing that impresses me most is not the playing stuff. I talk to Mike when I can when the Dodgers come in town and he's really stayed the same nice guy. There hasn't been a whole lot of change at all."

Whatever the future held, Mike Piazza had already become a legend in his own time as the player nobody wanted who made it to the top.

CHRONOLOGY

1968 Born Michael Joseph Piazza in Norristown, Pennsylvania on September 4

1988 Drafted No. 1,390 (out of 1,433 taken) in the Amateur Draft by the Los Angeles Dodgers

1991 Leads Dodgers farm system with 29 home runs while at Bakersfield

1992 Goes 3-for-3 in first major league game on September 1 at Chicago; Hits first big-league home run on September 12

1993 Plays in first of four consecutive All-Star Games; Unanimously wins National League "Rookie of the Year"

1996 Named All-Star Game Most Valuable Player; Tours Japan with Major League Baseball All-Stars

MAJOR LEAGUE STATISTICS

LOS ANGELES DODGERS

YEAR	TEAM	G	AB	R	H	2B	3B	HR	RBI	AVG	SB
1992	LA	21	69	5	16	3	0	1	7	.232	0
1993		149	547	81	174	24	2	35	112	.318	3
1994		107	405	64	129	18	0	24	92	.319	1
1995		112	434	82	150	17	0	32	93	.346	1
1996		148	547	87	184	16	0	36	105	.336	0
Totals		557	2002	319	653	78	2	128	409	.326	5

FURTHER READING

Cohen, Stanley. *The Dodgers: The First 100 Years.* New York: Carol Publishing Group, 1990.

Goodman, Michael. *Los Angeles Dodgers.* Mankato, MN: Creative Education, 1992.

Macht, Norman L. *Roy Campanella.* Philadelphia, PA: Chelsea House, 1996.

Sehnert, Chris W. *Los Angeles Dodgers.* Minneapolis: Abdo & Daughters, 1997.

INDEX

PICTURE CREDITS
Richard Lasner: p. 2; AP/Wide World Photos: pp. 8, 12, 17, 24, 32, 36, 38, 40, 42, 48, 50; National Baseball
Library and Archives, Cooperstown, NY: pp. 14, 46, 56, 58; Miami-Dade North CC: p. 20; The Sports Group: p. 26;
Dr. David K. Mulliken: p. 28; Transcendental Graphics: p. 54.

BRANT JAMES is a sports journalist who has dedicated eight years to watching, reporting, and enjoying baseball. A native of Maryland's Eastern Shore and a graduate of West Virginia University, James spent five years covering the Baltimore Orioles and minor league baseball for the Easton (MD) *Star-Democrat,* and now works in the sports department of the Baltimore *Sun.* He is currently working on a comprehensive biography of Hall of Fame slugger and fellow Eastern Shoreman Jimmie Foxx, and is based in Cockeysville, Maryland, near Baltimore.

JIM MURRAY, veteran sports columnist of the *Los Angeles Times,* is one of America's most acclaimed writers. He has been named "America's Best Sportswriter" by the National Association of Sportscasters and Sportswriters 14 times, was awarded the Red Smith Award, and was twice winner of the National Headliner Award. In addition, he was awarded the J. G. Taylor Spink Award in 1987 for "meritorious contributions to baseball writing." With this award came his 1988 induction into the National Baseball Hall of Fame in Cooperstown, New York. In 1990, Jim Murray was awarded the Pulitzer Prize for Commentary.

EARL WEAVER is the winningest manager in the Baltimore Orioles' history by a wide margin. He compiled 1,480 victories in his 17 years at the helm. After managing eight different minor league teams, he was given the chance to lead the Orioles in 1968. Under his leadership the Orioles finished lower than second place in the American League East only four times in 17 years. One of only 12 managers in big league history to have managed in four or more World Series, Earl was named Manager of the Year in 1979. The popular Weaver had his number, 5, retired in 1982, joining Brooks Robinson, Frank Robinson, and Jim Palmer, whose numbers were retired previously. Earl Weaver continues his association with the professional baseball scene by writing, broadcasting, and coaching.